STOWE
A VERMONT TOWN FOR ALL SEASONS

STOWE

A VERMONT TOWN FOR ALL SEASONS

STOWE
A VERMONT TOWN FOR ALL SEASONS

Photographs & Essays by

ORAH MOORE

Introduction by BIDDLE DUKE

HAYMAKER PRESS

Published by

First Edition
Copyright © 2011 by Orah Moore
All Rights Reserved

Book Design by Carrie Cook
Editing by Kathleen James

No part of this book may be reproduced or transmitted in any form or by any means,
electronic, mechanical, photocopying, recording, or otherwise, without prior consent of the publishers. For information,
please address Haymaker Press, P.O. Box 522, Morrisville, Vermont, 05661, or call 802-888-2309.

Printed in the USA by Capital Offset Company

ISBN: 978-0-9833271-0-3
Library of Congress Control Number: 2011910453

For information and book orders, visit our website:
www.HaymakerPress.com

Cover photograph: "Changing Seasons in Stowe, Vermont"

Dedicated to the memory of my parents, David and Nancy Ryder Moore

TABLE OF CONTENTS

Preface: The Light and the Land and My Camera, by Orah Moore   8

Introduction: Home in Stowe, by Biddle Duke   10

WINTER   14

MUD & SUGAR   48

SPRING   64

SUMMER   78

AUTUMN   98

WINTER REPRISE   120

End Notes   138

Acknowledgements   141

About the Artist   142

THE LIGHT AND THE LAND AND MY CAMERA *by Orah Moore*

I moved to the Stowe area in 1987 with my young family.

I had skied here as a child on many family holidays. Years later, just out of high school, I helped my mom and dad build a small cottage on Elmore Mountain Road that they could use for weekend getaways. Eventually they built their dream home for retirement on the same land.

Dad was an avid skier and an engineer. So building his own home in a land he dearly loved was pretty close to the best retirement he could have imagined. He first came to Stowe to ski as a young man in the 1940s, back in the days when a single chairlift hauled skiers up Mount Mansfield. I remember the arrival of the first triple chair, with heavy wool ponchos to help skiers stay (somewhat) warm during the long and slow ascent to the top.

Once my parents were living here full-time, Dad was out early almost every winter morning to make first tracks on the Front Four. He was not a good barometer of the actual ski conditions. If you asked him what it was like up on the mountain, he always had the same answer: "Great!" To get the real skinny on the weather, you would have to ask, "But how would your wife like the skiing today?" Then he might answer, "She would think it was too windy…or too cold…or too cloudy." But to my dad, the mountain was beloved, and every day he spent on it was a gift to his soul.

But winter is not the only season in Stowe. As a photographer, I am in love with every season, every day, every sunrise, every sunset.

I am often asked if I take my cameras with me everywhere. The answer is yes and no. Yes, I have my cameras with me more often than the average person might. But I'm not always able to stop and shoot—and sometimes, I've left my cameras at home. I miss some awesome opportunities. When that happens, I store the scene away in my mind.

There are two methods to my nature photography. One: I return often to the same route, to see new patterns of light on familiar scenes. Two: I scout out new routes, to see the light fall on unfamiliar scenes.

Stowe is a special place. It has a natural beauty because of how the land lays, nestled into the Mansfield mountain range and flanked by the Worcesters. And at a time when traditional main streets are disappearing, the village is truly lovely. Stowe has a mix of year-round locals, second-home owners, and once-a-year repeat visitors. Weekend travelers—or someone simply passing through—can't help but be struck by the charm and beauty of this place. Stowe also has a core of dedicated community members who organize amazing events, from outdoor recreation to arts and culture. It's a rare weekend when there is not more to do in Stowe than time to do it. The arts are alive in Stowe, with far more than the sound of music.

This book is my gift to the community. I may not portray every iconic view, nor every popular event. I also have included a few images that were shot in a neighboring town, or while standing in Stowe looking toward, for example, Elmore Mountain. My goal is to present the integrity and essence of Stowe in a well-rounded collection of seasonal images.

I have been photographing Stowe "in earnest" (as The Logger might say) since the day I moved here, when the long-gone Mayo Farm had its pigs eating leftovers from the Ben and Jerry's ice cream factory. ("They like every kind except the mint," a farmhand told me as I photographed the pigs slobbering over a bucket of strawberry.) I did not know then how entwined the light and the land and my camera would become for me. I just shoot—as often as possible.

Just like dad and his skiing: it's me and the light and the land and my camera.

INTRODUCTION: HOME IN STOWE *by Biddle Duke*

At some point after my family and I moved to Stowe in the late 1990s, I realized the noise I was waking to most mornings was a truck coming down from Paul Percy's farm.

We live at the bottom of Weeks Hill. Paul's farm is near the top. After the pre-dawn milking, one of his trucks heads our way. My head is still on the pillow when I hear its rumble, the sound of low-gear braking on the steep pitch half a mile away. The driver shifts up a gear or two as the road flattens by our driveway, and the engine quiets down. But the old house still gives a little shiver as the rig rushes past toward the village.

The Percy farm is one of five dairy farms in town. And one of the prettiest, perched on open farmland with a view in the distance of Mount Mansfield, the rolling Worcester Range, and the Stowe Community Church steeple poking up optimistically in the village below.

A few weeks after we moved to Stowe in the spring of 1998, my wife and I took our son and daughter, then about three and six, up for a look. It was a late spring afternoon and Paul was there with a helper, beginning the evening's milking. The big white-haired farmer was welcoming in that unimpressed New England way.

At some point he said something like, "So, why'd you buy the paper?" I'd bought the local weekly and a lot of people in town were wondering the same thing.

I fumbled for an answer. I was in the middle of a newspaper career, I said. I'd run papers for others, and now I wanted to do it for myself. I added: "I bought it so we could live down the hill from a dairy farm."

This amused Paul. "That's good." I didn't mention anything about the truck in the morning. I had a feeling that the sound of that truck every morning was a reason to feel good about life in Stowe, not the other way around.

Our old house started to be built sometime before the Civil War. I say "started to be built" because like any old wooden house in Vermont, the work never stops—it's been in an ongoing state of construction for almost 200 years, forever battered by wind and rain and snow, and forever being repainted and patched and expanded.

The house's defining feature is that it's on the road. Historically, that's where houses should be. Not much driveway to plow and in clear sight of the neighbors and passersby in case we need them or they need us. Being by the road made life easier. Still does.

It's also a responsibility and keeps us on our toes. The summer after we moved in, my wife came home one day to find a note on our door. It was from one of the Lepine sisters. Farmers and stewards of some of the most beautiful land in Vermont, just over the hill in Mud City, the three Lepines occasionally passed by our house on the way home.

We've since lost the note. I wish we'd framed it. I think of it now as a compliment. It said they hoped we'd restore an old historic barn on our property that had once belonged to the local school's shop teacher, Anson Page. We'd never given much thought to the crumbling building; we figured we'd let it slip into the earth. Now, it seemed, we couldn't. It was Anson Page's barn.

The Lepine note was one of those little moments when I realized we'd moved somewhere special. In my experience that realization doesn't come like a bolt of lightning; it comes gradually, over time.

We were gypsies before Stowe—South Carolina, Buenos Aires, New Mexico, New York—as I pursued the big story for newspapers in all of those places. Then we came here and our life changed, dramatically and beautifully. A decade slipped by in a flurry of raising children and making a living, and in what seemed like no time at all, we'd lived here longer than anyplace else.

Stowe was a fluke, really. I was working for a news company in South Carolina and in my spare time we'd looked at little newspapers in several states with an eye to buying and moving. But no place was quite right. Tiny weeklies were what we could afford.

We looked at interesting papers in neat communities in Maine, Montana and western North Carolina. But there was always something that didn't quite work: the schools, the local economy, the feel of the place.

So, where, honey? I asked my wife Idoline. A University of Vermont graduate, she replied: "Anywhere in Vermont."

As it turned out, I knew Trow Elliman. He owned the *Stowe Reporter*. I had dated his niece long ago, and I was her date at Trow's daughter's wedding. When I called him 15 years later, he said he remembered me, though I doubt it.

I'd been to Vermont as a New Hampshire ski racer in my teens and on that one June wedding weekend. But I didn't know Vermont. It took one visit in the winter of 1998, when we came to see if this was the place, to feel the gentle tug of it. We arrived on a blue-sky February day, the snow thick on eves and roadsides. We'd missed real winter for many years, and the wood smoke, the skis and snowboards on the cars, the sight of our breath, the friendly newspaper and candy merchant on Main Street, all of that swept over us like a wave of happy memories. Places like this still exist, I found myself remarking.

I bought the paper, and we moved. Years have passed and I'm still learning about Vermont, its myths and its magic, its sense of being both connected and disconnected from the rest of New England. Its independent people, its tight, self-reliant communities. Its five or six distinct, wonderful and infuriating seasons that keep coming, often not in sequence, like last May when it snowed, and some Januaries when the crocuses start punching through the ice crust. Vermont is close horizons and frank, unemotional people. It is looking out at a little sun in the morning and saying "seize it now." Because it won't last.

Stowe is all that—but almost 200 years of visitors have brought change. Yet the community's core remains intact; many of the descendants of the town's earliest settlers are among the town's central figures, serving on local boards and speaking up at Town Meeting every March. Stowe is forever changing with younger and new residents taking the lead and old-timers stepping back.

But that's how it's always been. Consider the mid-1800s, when William H. H. Bingham, a Stowe lawyer and politician, recognized the area as a gem and began to develop the town for visitors. By 1860, Bingham had built the 200-room Mansfield Hotel on Main Street (since burned down) and the Summit House (removed half a century ago) near the top of the mountain, accessible by horse-drawn carriage up the Toll Road.

The two hotels, the road and the views from the summit thrust Stowe into the spotlight. Some called it the Saratoga of Vermont, and on some summer days its population of about 600—mostly loggers and sheep farmers—would swell with as many as 500 guests. In 1870, by one count, 1,000 people traveled up the Toll Road by foot and horse and carriage. Those days are not so far removed from today, when our town of about 4,300 doubles in population—or more—on busy summer and winter weekends.

Stowe remains a destination for visitors from around the world, but to live here is to know that it's a community first, a tiny New England village, with its town hall and an inn on Main Street and an excellent library.

"Skiing initially brought us here, but Stowe's lifestyle and beauty kept us here," art gallery owner Scott Noble remarked to me recently. Noble moved here about a decade ago and has taken a lead in Stowe affairs.

David Rocchio, an attorney and columnist in my newspaper and a friend, grew up in the Mad River Valley but decided to move here with his wife to raise their family.

"Since I was a child Stowe has changed tremendously," he told me. "Since 9/11 it has changed as much again. As long as we keep in mind what makes this town so vibrant and special—true community, a small village that's not overly commercial, beautiful working landscape, open lands and plenty of mountain to play on—it will, through all the change, be a wonderful place to call home, raise a family…and maybe blow off work and ski in the morning now and again."

Orah Moore and I have been working together for more than a decade. Well, working together in a manner of speaking. Her remarkable photographs of the life and landscape of this area regularly appear in the magazine that I publish, *The Stowe Guide*. Orah has had many lives in many places, and has captured all of them with her lens. But this is home, and has been for many years, and you can feel it in her photographs.

I've ridden my bicycle to work everywhere I've lived, even through the streets of Buenos Aires, where it was a risky act of defiance. Miraculously, I live to write about it. I ride to work here, but not in defiance. I see friends along the way; I stop and have a coffee; I run into neighbors, and into conversations that I had left a day or a week before.

"How is Biddle Duke these days?" It is my neighbor and farmer Paul Percy. I've called him for advice. We haven't spoken in over a year but we're talking as if recently interrupted. We talk about farming, and he tells me something amazing: Although there are fewer farms in Stowe than at any time since dairy took hold here, the town's remaining farmers are producing more milk than ever, thanks to efficient farming techniques and milking machines and more productive cows.

"I could come down and talk to you about that," says Paul, with pride. His Jerseys and Holsteins are responsible for the lion's share of the town's milk output.

"It's a good story," I reply, and I detect in me something unfamiliar. Pride. About my hometown. About the volume of milk being produced in my hometown. Who would have thought?

I sleep later these days. Our kids have grown up and there's no rush to get them off to school in the morning. The 6 a.m. truck from the Percy farm still rumbles past. But I stopped hearing it long ago.

—*Biddle Duke*

Biddle Duke bought the Stowe Reporter *in May of 1998. The newspaper celebrated 50 years of continuous weekly publication in 2008 and has been awarded best community weekly in Vermont by the Vermont Press Association for many years running.*

WINTER

stretches loosely over six months in Stowe. It sputters and stutters in November, with shorter and shorter days. It teases in December, as we count down to the solstice, but we usually have a white Christmas and several good days of skiing. The bone-chilling cold and clear starry nights of January hold the snowpack between the occasional thaw.

...MORE LIGHT.

February is fickle, with big blizzards followed by dry spells. It's the finest time to be outside. We snowshoe and ski, downhill and cross country, as often as we possibly can.

...MORE LIGHT. MORE SNOW.

March is usually reliable for sunshine and snow. The sap begins to run. Trees get tapped, buckets get filled and emptied. Lines get checked, and the boiling starts, bringing the sweet smell and taste of maple syrup. Liquid gold.

...MORE LIGHT. LONGER DAYS. MORE!

Then there is April, the month of transition. Some of us grow weary of winter, while others relish the last days of spring skiing. Still others are nurturing seedlings inside, waiting for the promised spring.

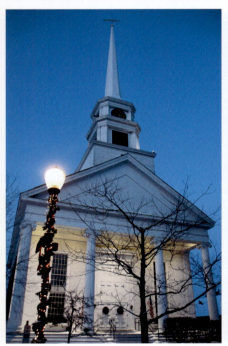

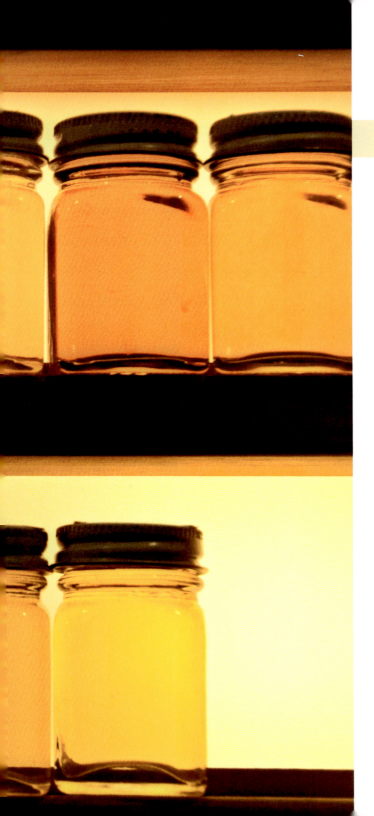

MUD & SUGAR

season sneaks in come March, when the snow is still flying but the temperatures bounce up, causing short sleeves to be donned for a few hours. The season plays with us—and sends sugarmakers into a tizzy, with starts and stops in the sap runs. Will it be a good year for making syrup? Will it be better than last year or worse? Will those extra taps play out?

Will the syrup be mostly FANCY, or start with MEDIUM AMBER right out of the tree? And will the truck make it through the mud?

Speaking of mud…I recently called the Stowe highway department to ask about the most notoriously muddy road in town. I wanted to get some really good mud and pothole shots, and in recent years, I just haven't been able to find those sections guaranteed to suck your car into a 10-inch rut and make steering all but impossible. Just over the border in Waterbury or Elmore? Sure, I know those places. But where in Stowe proper?

Nowhere, apparently. "We fill the holes as soon as we find them," they said. "We have our own gravel pit!"

Now that is just no fun.

But it does make it easier to get to the sugarhouses for another nip of HOT, FANCY, LIQUID GOLD.

SPRING

in Stowe is a gift, our reward for making it through another long season of cold and white. Green begins to assert itself in April. Every shoot, every bud is green, but not summer green: spring green.

IT'S SPRING GREEN, LIME GREEN, BUDDING GREEN, NEWBORN GREEN.

April and May are the unidentical twin-sister months of spring.

April has one foot in winter and one foot in spring. And at some point every crocus and daffodil, and even the tulips, may briefly wear a coat of snowy white.

But green marches on. It shrugs off the white and does not look back.

May has one foot in spring and one foot in summer. It's a perfect match. May is delightful, with brilliant shades of green, fields full of dandelions, and welcome warm weather. Early gardens get started. Late frosts threaten and then recede, reassuring us that summer will soon be here.

SUMMER

seems so brief in Stowe that we immediately embrace it, squeezing every wakeful moment out of June, July and August.

WE CELEBRATE.

The summer light vibrates with every color in nature's palette: green grass, red barns and blue sky. Multi-colored hot-air balloons grace the sky. Cows graze the pastures. Gardens bloom.

WE CELEBRATE.

Hikers, bikers and runners explore every square inch of Stowe's mountains and trails. We get outside.

AND WE CELEBRATE.

Enjoy the annual two-day August heat wave, or complain about it. Then blink and summer is gone, as autumn slips in.

AUTUMN

is the signature season in Stowe.
It is beauty in its most concentrated and compact form.

There's a twinge of panic in late summer that stretches into early fall, when the first maple leaf turns red on an otherwise green tree. Soon it will be cold. We accept it. And then we glide through late fall that stretches into early winter, when the last yellow poplar leaf lets go of an otherwise naked tree.

But autumn, sometimes sharply defined as fall foliage season—that high-energy time when thousands arrive in our fair land—is really only about one thing:

PEAK COLOR.

It's two, three, maybe four days at the most. The color is full force and high octane, at times so surreal that one tourist asked me, "Did they paint the leaves red?" Yes, "they" did. Every single leaf—

RED, CRIMSON, ORANGE, UMBER AND GOLD.

Peak foliage is a thing of wonder. It's intense…and then it is gone. Silence. Except for the wind whistling through the empty limbs as we collectively turn toward winter once again.

WINTER REPRISE

The green of spring has come and gone. Summer's carefree embrace has ended. Autumn's vivid mountainside mural has faded. And winter is upon us again.

We live in the North because we love winter. Not the subzero temperatures, not the pipes that freeze and break, not the relentless plowing and shoveling and roof-raking.

WE LOVE THE WHITE.

We endure stick season while we wait for the snow. Big flakes and sunshine: it doesn't get much better than that.

END NOTES

WINTER

1. "Harvest Time" (The Ricketson's Farm) is on Route 100, with Elmore Mountain rising above the cornstalks.
2. The trails on Mount Mansfield call out to skiers.
4. "Scottish Highlanders" wintering at Trapp Family Lodge.
5. My parents loved skiing at Stowe. This early sunrise on a crisp winter morning would have seen my dad first in line at the quad. "Mount Mansfield Revealed."
6. "Green Woods in Stowe Hollow" shot on a misty, magical morn.
8. "Rainbow Balloons" rise above the Stoweflake Festival, with "Fireworks Against Blue," "Steeple through the Oak Leaves" (Stowe Community Church) and the Notch from the Octagon deck (section of "Mount Mansfield Panoramic").
10. Stowe downtown as seen from a plane, with Percy's Jersey cows, light slicing across Mayo's field and the bike that's a permanent fixture outside the *Stowe Reporter* office.
12. "Stowe, Vermont," a classic village with the mountain rising above.
14. "Sleigh Ride at Trapps" was taken just at dusk, with Deb Ravenelle driving Burt and Rex and a couple enjoying the night.
16. Dawn arrives quietly as you enter Stowe coming north on Route 100, with the Stowe Maple Products sugarhouse in the background. Chairlifts awaiting service.
18. Early in the winter, before last year's cornstalks get covered, a bus is seen "Heading to School."
20. A medley of winter evenings after a layer of snow settles on home and barn and church.
21. "Stowe Storm" says patience to me. An early morning hike up to Sunset Rock after a heavy snowstorm revealed dull gray everywhere. After 30 minutes of waiting, the sky turned an amazing shade of steel blue.
22. Holiday time in Stowe is special. Buildings and lampposts get decorated, trees get chosen and cut at Paine's Tree Farm, and always there is more shoveling to do! (Jeff Dezotell is clearing the walk in front of Shaw's General Store.)
24. The theme in these photos is wreaths and fir trees. On the left is "Wreath on the Historic Ide House." Think of the snow-covered tires as a unique type of winter wreath!
26. "Winter Glow" was shot very early one December morning, five days before Christmas. "Holiday Magic in Vermont" depicts the steps of the Memorial Building on Main Street.
28. "Vermont Village" (Stowe) was also shot from Sunset Rock. Evening's arrival is one of my favorite times to shoot in a village. As the sky fades to deep blue, the streetlights come on.
30. "The Ski Museum at Midnight" stands out in this Edward Hopper-style image of dramatic night light. In contrast, "Night Magic at Trapps" is lit up, sparkly and gay and inviting.
32. After ushering at a late show at Spruce Peak Performing Arts Center, I stood in the parking lot just after midnight and marveled at the full moon, lodge and mountain. What fortune that I had my camera and tripod in the car that night and took "Midnight Moonlight at the Lodge." By contrast, a quiet shot of a lone car on Weeks Hill Road, shot before daybreak on "The Winter Solstice."
34. "Virgin Corduroy!" The trees are swathed in snow and more snow.
36. Mary Johnson, ski instructor with local school programs, playing in the woods.
38. "Stowe Mountain Panoramic"... Wow! It was an amazing day to photograph (and ski) at the Mountain. The quad. Rick Howell skiing at Spruce Peak. The Stone Hut.
40. Top to bottom: Trapps instructors, Sam von Trapp in the Stowe Derby and a lone snowshoer (Sally Stetson) "Heading towards Camel's Hump." Marc Gilbertson, Vermont's Nagano Olympics cross-country skier, manages to get the number "1" bib in the Stowe Derby once again! Backdrop: Stowe Mountain, Stoweflake and the Jewish Community Center of Greater Stowe.
42. Without fail we see our share of winter storms in Stowe. "Emily's Bridge During a Storm," offers shelter for a few covered yards!
44. And after every storm comes a beautiful day: "The Rec Path Bridge;" a lone cross-country skier (Ginger Huber) takes advantage of the fresh snow; the "Footbridge on the Mountain Road." "After the Storm" was shot looking toward Stowe Hardware.
46. "Silent Night" sees Stowe into the evening and "Elmore Mountain Sunrise" sends out a wake-up call: It is a new day in Stowe, Vermont!

MUD AND SUGAR

48. Potholes on Dewey Hill Road and a collection of maple syrup grade testers at Nebraska Knoll Sugarhouse.

50 Frank Kellogg has been sugaring for the past 50 years, gathering sap in his woods with a yoke he made, and boiling in a shed out back. In a good year, he gets eight gallons. Also: Stowe road crew repairing the spring roads.

52 There is plenty of mud on the way to Nason Adams' sugarhouse. He and his son Ed work the sugarhouse the time-honored way, with wood.

54 Nebraska Knoll Sugarhouse sends up sparks into the dusk as they work into the night to keep up with a good run. Also: liquid gold being poured off.

56 Sugaring seems like a spring thing, but it gets going while the snow is still around. Sometimes it gets so cold that the boiling stops for days—and then starts again as the roads thaw and the days warm up after cold nights.

58 Nebraska Knoll Sugarhouse, owned by Lewis and Audrey Coty, is a true community gathering place. On long boiling nights, they get plenty of help from the neighbors.

60 I visited Paul Percy on a day so snowy that the sugarhouse was almost invisible from the field. I asked Paul, "What is your favorite grade of syrup?" His reply: "Is there anything but fancy?" 'Nuf said.

61 Steve Pierson of Stowe Maple Products is pretty much a one-man-band of nonstop boiling energy. His sugar wood is not next to his sugarhouse, so he gathers by truck.

62 Trapps has its sugarhouse nestled in the woods, so cross-country skiers can stop in to see the boiling. All gathering is done by horse, and the sugarhouse is run by Hal and Alex without the aid of electricity, so no boiling goes on after dark.

SPRING

64 "Main Street Rainbow," along with glistening green.

66 Sometimes after the tulips are up and the trees start to bud, we get hit with an amazing snowstorm. But it leaves as fast as it comes, because the ground is spring-warm. "Late Spring Storm at Trapps."

68 The Spear Farm. Elizabeth Squier, Stowe's Aussie shepherdess, with her new spring lambs. (Top right: "Jump for Joy." Bottom right: "Sweet Kid.")

70 "Moss Glen Falls," young beech leaves in the woods, the road up through Smugglers' Notch and "Blossoming Under Elmore" explode into shades of green.

72 More signs of spring: Newborn birds, "Purple Lilacs," "Woodland Slippers" (pink ladies' slippers) and buds.

74 Planting corn on the Ricketson's farmland.

76 A couple at night in Stowe and "Night Sky over Trapps."

SUMMER

78 Barns—although not all are "working barns"—are still situated around every bend in the road. ("A Mid Summer's Day.")

80 Stoweflake Resort has been hosting a balloon fest for more than 25 years in Stowe. ("Balloons Over Stowe" and "Four Balloons in Vermont.")

82 The Trapp meadow is home to summer concerts and pre-concert picnics.

84 Stowe puts on one of the best Fourth of July fireworks displays in the state, in my humble opinion. ("Red Night" and "Fireworks with Barn.")

86 The longtime home of the Lackeys on Main Street and their classic Lackey's Variety Store, now owned by Susan Spera. And it's always a pleasure to stop in to McCarthy's for breakfast or lunch. Shown here are Lee LaBier at the counter and long-time waitress Jill Warner serving up my eggs. Also: "The Spear Barn" and "Gold Brook Covered Bridge."

88 Paul Percy's "Jersey Girls" and his Weeks Hill farm, as referred to in the book's introduction by Biddle Duke. The pigs are from long ago, when the Mayo Farm was still a working farm. My title for the pigs in my line of greeting cards is "Harriet and Wilbur."

90 This photo spread is a journey through Stowe Hollow. If you get lost driving around back there, you will see these views. Also: Gold Brook covered bridge (also known as Emily's Bridge). "Stowe Hollow Road."

92 "The Trapp Family Lodge" and gardens are always a treat to visit, and I have shot many a wedding there. (Elmore Mountain is shown in the background.)

94 Stowe Land Trust has preserved this barn overlooking the Pinnacle, now in the mist. It is part of the Grandview Farm, conserved in 1996. Also: "Evening" as seen from the Trapp meadow at a concert.

96 "The Valley Awakening" shows Elmore Mountain, as the fog dissipates and the sun rises on the Trapp gardens.

AUTUMN

98 The Stowe Community Church ("Autumn in Stowe, Vermont") is a landmark building that says "Stowe" from just about every direction in the community.

100 "Autumn in Vermont" has been a best-selling poster for me for years. I think it is ironic that there is no barn and no church steeple and it breaks all the rules about a well-composed photo—and yet…it works. "Resting Cow" takes a break with Mount Mansfield as her backdrop. Not a bad view for her.

102 "Steeple Through the Oak Leaves," "Abstract Autumn," the hardware store, and the Parker barn on West Hill Road.

104 This spread is a study in yellow, with the Stowe Hollow dirt road, the road into Smugglers' Notch, the famous rock passage, tourists getting a shot of yellow trees, and a sign at a trailhead for the Pinnacle.

106 "Fall Beauty." On the right is the Grandview Farm, shown with "The Pinnacle" in the background—a fabulous place to hike in the fall.

108 "Bingham Falls" off the Mountain Road, and "Hidden Waterfall" in the Notch that is often out of view.

110 After the Stowe Foliage Arts Festival at Topnotch Field. Route 100 heading north takes in the Ricketson Farm and Elmore Mountain.

112 A medley of fall, wild apples, "Red Maple," early fall and "Splash of Color."

114 "Harvest Wagon," "Pie Pumpkins," "Carved Pumpkins" and Adams' pumpkin field.

116 Some years we get a lovely early snowstorm before the leaves have fallen. When this happens, the Notch gets closed due to icy conditions near the top. Shown with the gondola, "Winter Visits Fall in Stowe."

118 Canada geese finally head south, but "Crow on a Wire" holds out for a bit longer.

WINTER REPRISE

120 I have photographed the mountain so often from Edson Hill, but never before from this vantage point. "Mansfield Awakes."

122 "Dawn on the Mountain" in Stowe, in the winter, never ceases to leave me in awe. I stand and watch as the sun sweeps down from the ridgeline, painting the blue into pink. A second photo, taken several years earlier yet with a similar feel, is "Stowe Village Sunrise."

124 "Winter Fence in the Hollow" and "Stowe at Dawn" with muted and mellow morning light.

126 My mother asked me to make her a snowman. But it was a fluffy-snow day! So on the next wet-snow day, I made her this fellow, called "Winter Friend." On the right is the beautiful red-brick house on the corner of Route 100 and the Mountain Road.

128 Winter is monochromatic, so when I see colors I feel compelled to shoot. Most of these photos came from a walk around the town, going behind the buildings. Left: "Steeple Through the Trees." Top right: Stowe Historical Society building. Bottom right: a mother and daughter walking to church.

130 "The West Branch River" on the left and "Mansfield Shining in the Dawn" on the right.

132 "Behold, Winter!" with Mansfield in the distance, "The New Lodge," the road to get there, and Spruce Peak.

134 Sandy and Gen Thompson snowshoeing with the family. Patty Hammer and her dog, Paco, walking in Wiessner Woods, conserved in 1992.

136 "Morning Whisper" and "Silence in Blue." What more is there to say?

END NOTES & ACKNOWLEDGEMENTS

139 Friday Women's Hockey League: "Want to join, Orah?" they asked me.

140 "Edson Hill Road Pond."

141 Lyndall Heyer, ready to transplant the tomatoes; "Concert in the Rain" in Trapp Meadow that brought out the umbrellas; red on red; "Dawn on Edson Hill."

144 "So long, farewell…" A giant sunflower in the Trapp gardens.

Acknowledgements

I feel privileged to have worked with "Team Stowe Book" as I refer to them: Carrie Cook, a talented and tireless designer of everything graphic and visual in this book; Jo Sabel-Courtney, my marketing and PR manager extraordinaire, who loves this project almost as much as I do; Kathleen James, former editor of *Vermont Magazine*, with whom I have worked for more than four years and trust implicitly; Peter Cook, printer liaison, who helped me to navigate the world of ink and paper; Biddle Duke, for his words of encouragement and willingness to write an introduction out of sheer love of Stowe; Ward Rice, who has printed my photographs exquisitely for over 24 years and is always willing to help me make a better print.

More thanks go to Dylan Fetterman, Taylor Fetterman, Dana Billingsley, Dianne Schwartz, Ansel Adams (my mentor of many years ago), Cooksey-Talbott, Mary Johnson, Jennifer Ranz, Gail Wheel, Pat Haslam, Sherry Baraw, David Budbill, Rusty DeWees, Colyn Case, Susan Adams, Kathy Wilder, Amanda Kuhnert, Ginger Huber, Glenn Callahan, Karl Schoff and everyone whom I photographed in connection with this book.

ABOUT THE ARTIST

PHOTO: COURTESY OF A STOWE TOURIST

I invited my friend Orah Moore to supper one night last winter. She called around sunset to say she'd be late, for a reason I could have guessed: she was working.

Orah is almost always working, which is one of the things I admire about her. She had paused on the way to my house, stopped by the sight of the Big Dipper rising above a church spire. Her camera was ready; could dinner wait? I assured her it could.

Another time when Orah came to supper, several years earlier, I'd made the mistake of asking her to "snap a few quick shots" of my oldest daughter. The favor turned into an hour-long portrait session. My youngest daughter was called into duty as a photographer's assistant, holding up a blank poster board to serve as a makeshift backdrop.

The portraits were perfect, which is always Orah's goal. I had hired her as a photographer many times when I was editor of *Vermont Magazine,* and several times had to politely encourage her to call it quits. "The pictures you sent are great," I'd say. "We have more than we need. You don't have to shoot any more." "OK," she'd say, with a vague tone that told me she wasn't paying attention. A few days later, a new CD would arrive at my office, filled with even better shots.

Orah grew up in Syracuse and attended Principia Upper School in St. Louis. After high-school graduation, she decided to postpone college because she wanted to get to work. During those early adult years, she reconnected with photography, a childhood hobby. "I was so attached to my camera that I could hardly see without it," she says. "So I set it aside for several years. I had to learn to see without it, to make peace with it. When I picked up my camera again, it was a balanced part of my life." Orah would live her life, rather than observe it—yet with her camera in hand, every day would offer the chance to celebrate what she sees.

Orah eventually returned to school and, over time, earned a master's degree in fine art photography from California State University at Fullerton. She also studied in Yosemite with Ansel Adams, whom she calls a "major influence." "He was known for his black-and-white fine-art photography, but he was also a commercial photographer," she says. "He worked hard but remained dedicated to his family. That balance impressed me."

Orah's resumé shows an unbroken succession of photography awards, exhibitions and published images, from the late 1970s through today. "I've shown my work somewhere—from galleries to art centers to the inside of an elevator—almost every year since 1977," she says. "The idea of showing is not to impress; it's to create something. It's also because I'm goal-oriented. Preparing for a show keeps my work focused and up-to-date."

While Orah is often in motion, she is purposeful rather than restless. Her images are the same: light and land, energy and emotion, caught in a single reflective frame. "My life is about seeing, creativity and order," she says. "These elements come together in the frame of a photograph, but the process starts long before I bring the lens to my eye. I wait for the elements to line up—form, composition, light. With or without a camera, I see in freeze frames."

Much of her photography documents the people and landscapes of Vermont, where she spent childhood vacations and has lived and raised her two sons, now adults, since 1987. That same year, she started a small business—Haymaker Press—to sell her photos as posters and greeting cards. In 2000, she moved her business to a storefront in downtown Morrisville; in addition to Haymaker Press, it also houses her retail gift shop, portrait studio and busy wedding-photography business. "Art and business have an intimate connection, not only for myself, but for the communities I work in," she says. "A good deal of my living has been made in Stowe. The community supports my work on many levels, and in turn, I want my work to support the community. Creating a book about the town seemed a fitting way to say thank you."

"'As the sowing, so the reaping' is a motto I've grown up with. This idea permeates my life and my business ethic," she says. "Sow kindness, reap kindness. Sow peace and balance, reap the same. I infuse my photographic efforts with these concepts. I find images with a sense of place…. Many of my photographs are of earth, sky and water—simple things accessible to all." That philosophy is reflected in Orah's work, and in her life.

—*Kathleen James*

"So long, farewell..."